Piano Solo

CHRISTMAS
TIDINGS

10 CAROL SETTINGS BY JOHN LEAVITT

ISBN 978-1-4803-3999-6

HAL•LEONARD®
CORPORATION

7777 W. BLUEMOUND RD. P.O. BOX 13819 MILWAUKEE, WI 53213

In Australia Contact:
Hal Leonard Australia Pty. Ltd.
4 Lentara Court
Cheltenham, Victoria, 3192 Australia
Email: ausadmin@halleonard.com.au

Visit Hal Leonard Online at
www.halleonard.com

CONTENTS

COVENTRY CAROL

Words by Robert Croo
Traditional English Melody
Arranged by John Leavitt

Cantabile espressivo ♩ = ca. 82

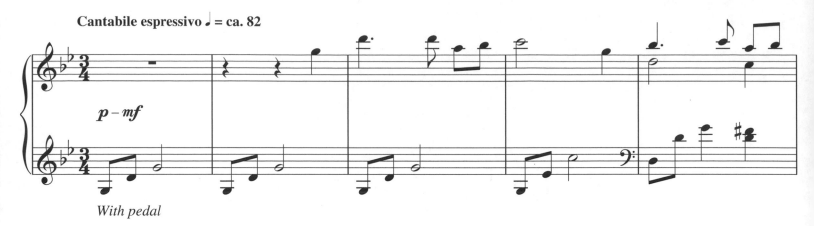

With pedal

To Coda

cresc. poco a poco

DECK THE HALL

Traditional Welsh Carol
Arranged by John Leavitt

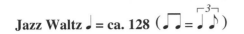

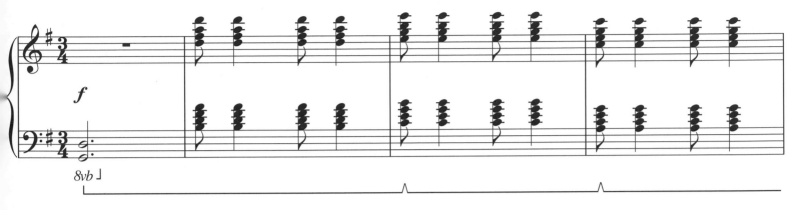

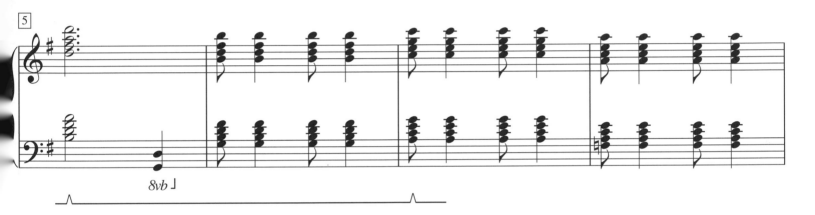

HE IS BORN, THE HOLY CHILD

(Il Est Ne, Le Divin Enfant)

Traditional French Carol
Arranged by John Leavitt

Sprightly ♩ = ca. 76

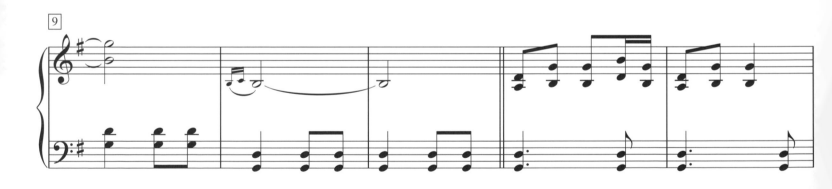

SING WE NOW OF CHRISTMAS

Traditional French Carol
Arranged by John Leavitt

Brightly ♩ = ca. 104

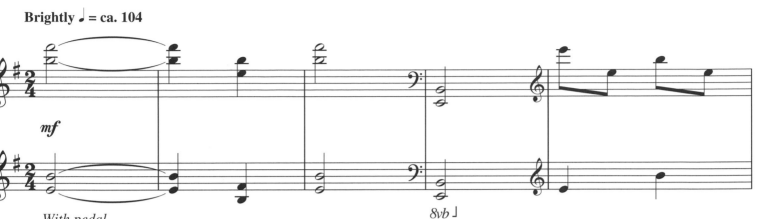

THE HOLLY AND THE IVY

18th Century English Carol
Arranged by John Leavitt

Moderately ♩ = ca. 104

mp

With pedal

O CHRISTMAS TREE

Traditional German Carol
Arranged by John Leavitt

With lyric simplicity ♩ = ca. 76

O HOLY NIGHT

French Words by Placide Cappeau
English Words by John S. Dwight
Music by Adolphe Adam
Arranged by John Leavitt

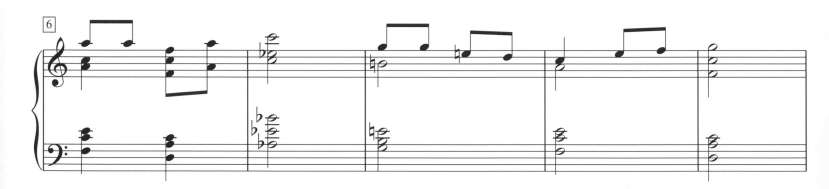

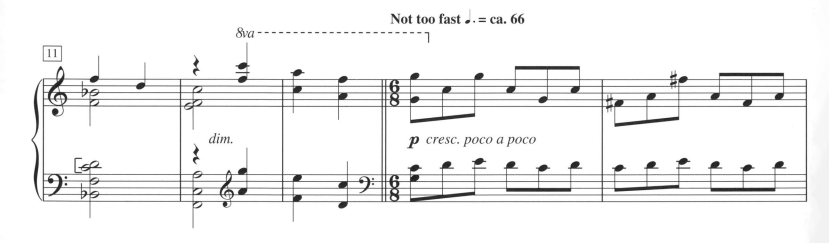

TOMORROW SHALL BE MY DANCING DAY

Traditional
Arranged by John Leavitt

Playfully ♩. = ca. 60

WHILE BY MY SHEEP

Traditional German Carol
Arranged by John Leavitt

Dance-like, with spirit ♩ = ca. 100

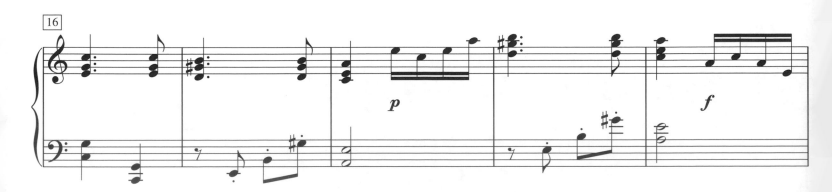

STILL, STILL, STILL

Salzburg Melody, c.1819
Traditional Austrian Text
Arranged by John Leavitt